IMAGES
of America

NEW ORLEANS

IMAGES
of America

NEW ORLEANS

Eric J. Brock

ARCADIA
PUBLISHING

Copyright © 1999 by Eric J. Brock
ISBN 978-0-7385-0223-6

Published by Arcadia Publishing
Charleston, South Carolina

Printed in the United States of America

Library of Congress Catalog Card Number applied for.

For all general information contact Arcadia Publishing at:
Telephone 843-853-2070
Fax 843-853-0044
E-Mail sales@arcadiapublishing.com
For customer service and orders:
Toll-Free 1-888-313-2665

Visit us on the Internet at www.arcadiapublishing.com

CONTENTS

Jean Baptiste le Moyne, Sieur de Bienville, founded the city of New Orleans in May 1718. Bienville named the city in honor of Philippe II, Duc d'Orleans, then Regent of King Louis XV. Born in Canada in 1680, Bienville first set foot in Louisiana in 1699. He served four times as colonial governor and worked tirelessly to make the Louisiana colony a success. In 1743 he moved to France, and died in Paris in 1768. The capital of the vast colony of Louisiana, Nouvelle Orleans, as it was first known, remained under French control until 1762, when it passed into Spanish hands under the terms of the Treaty of Fontainebleau. In 1800, through the treaty of San Ildefonso, France regained Louisiana, although no formal notification was given to the colonists until 1803, the same year the Emperor Napoleon sold the Louisiana Territory to the United States in the monumental land deal known as the Louisiana Purchase.

INTRODUCTION

New Orleans. Few cities anywhere can boast so rich a heritage. Since its founding in 1718, New Orleans has grown from being a backwater outpost of France to being one of the world's major cities. Possessed off and on by France, Spain, and finally by the United States, the spirit of the city blends the best elements of all three great cultures, making it unique in all of North America.

It has been said that New Orleans is the most Latin city in the United States. Quite so. In many respects the city has more in common culturally with Havana, Managua, or Cartagena than it does with any place in the U.S. Here one can still find exotic names for streets and neighborhoods—and for many of the inhabitants as well. There are foods that are seldom found elsewhere that are commonly found here. We experience weather that is fantastically tropical, and find old buildings suited especially to such climes.

New Orleans is famous for many things: "iron lace" on its historic buildings, cemeteries built above ground, jazz, creole cuisine, poboys, muffaletta sandwiches, fine French restaurants, cotton, sugar, one of the world's greatest ports, streetcars, Mardi Gras, romance, decadence, exuberance . . . It is a city with a soul—a very tangible, visible soul.

In 1803 New Orleans was the catalyst for perhaps the greatest land deal in the history of the world: the Louisiana Purchase. The United States wanted only New Orleans, but got what is now the entire central portion of the country in the bargain. A third of the present continental United States was acquired in order to obtain this one city. Why? Because of the Mississippi River. The control of the great river and its commerce was always the reason for the city's desirability by so many empires. Indeed, the river is the reason New Orleans exists at all. It is the reason the city was founded, the reason it grew, and the reason it remains today as one of the world's major trade centers. The Mississippi River and the city of New Orleans are intimately linked.

Of all of New Orleans's nicknames, the oldest and best known refers to its location on the Mississippi: the Crescent City. Situated on a great bend of the Mississippi River, the city's entire plan is based upon that location. Streets here do not run north, south, east, and west, but rather run parallel to or away from the river. On the opposite side of the city is Lake Pontchartrain, a massive but relatively shallow body of water. Between the river and the lake lies the main body of New Orleans, built upon what was once an inhospitable swamp, reclaimed by the hand of man over the past three centuries. Directions are often given as "lakeside" (in the direction of Lake Pontchartrain) or "riverside" (in the direction of the Mississippi). "Uptown" and "downtown" refer to the opposing directions: "uptown" being all that lies to the left of Canal Street if one stands with one's back to the river, and "downtown" being that which lies to its right.

Canal Street is one of the great thoroughfares of America. Once it divided the French Quarter from the American Sector, as the Central Business District was known in earlier times. The median of the street was known as the "neutral ground"—neither French nor American. It has been said that the meeting of the two cultures was often hostile, but this is greatly exaggerated. Certainly there was tension in the early days, but New Orleans has, almost from the beginning, been a very inclusive city. All religions and races have played major roles in the shaping of New Orleans, and for the most part, all have cooperated to build important communities here.

How many cities can boast three of the nation's most important and well-known streets? In New Orleans there is not only Canal Street, but also St. Charles Avenue and Bourbon Street. And Basin Street, Esplanade, and Magazine Street are only slightly less famous. Who in the nation has not heard of the French Quarter? Who has not heard of the Garden District? Who does not know the Superdome? New Orleans is imprinted on the mind of America in a thousand ways.

The Crescent City, also known as "The Big Easy" and "The City That Care Forgot," claimed the title of "America's Most Interesting City" for decades. While true, the motto lacked the short, pithy quality of New York's "Big Apple," Dallas' "Big D," or Chicago's "Windy City." "The Big Easy" came about quite by accident when a writer for the *New Orleans States-Item* compared the city's laid-back lifestyle to New York's, jokingly dubbing it "The Big Easy" as opposed to "The Big Apple." Shortly thereafter, in 1970, a crime novel set in New Orleans was given the title, "The Big Easy." Years later the novel was made into a movie and the slogan became a nationally recognized nickname for New Orleans.

What the city is called, however, makes little difference. It is a beautiful and extraordinary place with a rich and unusual heritage. This book provides a glimpse into that heritage through historic photographs of New Orleans, images of the city as it was, and, in some cases, as it still is. For all its diverse cultural legacy and for all that has been preserved, much also has been lost. This volume neither attempts nor pretends to be a thorough compendium of the sights or history of New Orleans. There are literally thousands of places, people, sights, and events that could be part of such a work, but due to space constraints and a lack of suitable images, they cannot be included here. A city as large and old as New Orleans simply cannot be summarized in a book of this length—or of any length. Rather, this is intended to be a celebration of the city's past, a whirlwind tour of the "Beautiful Crescent" through historic images.

One

THE VIEUX CARRE

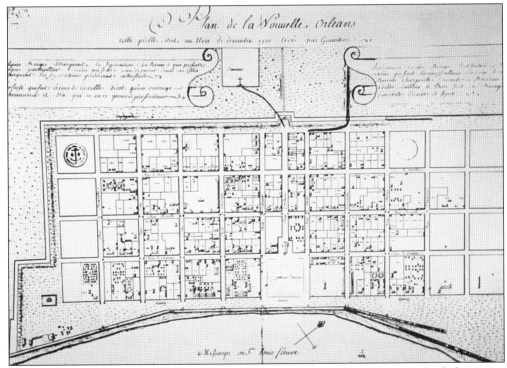

The *Vieux Carre*, or "Old Quarter," is the historic name for the area also commonly known as the French Quarter. It is the original town of New Orleans as laid out by the French engineer Adrien de Pauger in 1721. Prior to Pauger's arrival, New Orleans had been merely a random scattering of huts and crude buildings. By 1731, when this map was made, New Orleans' boundaries were roughly those of the present French Quarter. The built-up portion of the town then extended only as far back as Dauphine Street; beyond the edge of town was forest and the swamp.

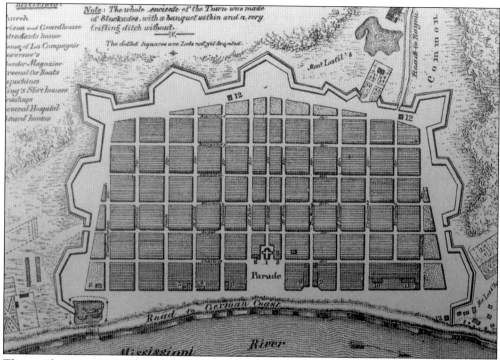

The rapid expansion of the original townsite under the U.S. regime is evidenced by these two maps. This view shows the city at the time of the American takeover in 1803. Clearly marked are the Spanish fortifications surrounding the city, which included five forts and ramparts along the townsite's borders. Rampart Street, back of the Quarter, takes its name from these defensive works. By 1803 they were falling into disrepair and were soon to be removed.

This 1815 map of the city shows the faubourgs (suburbs) that had grown up around the original site. Images of public buildings appear in the margins.

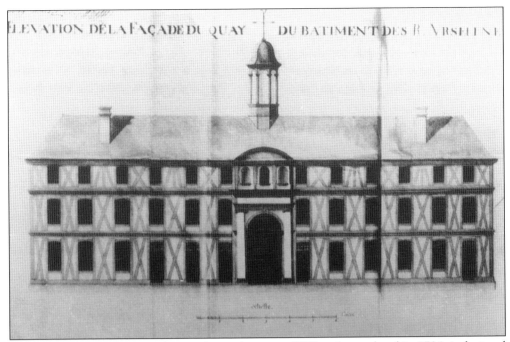

The Ursuline Convent on Chartres Street, begun in 1727 and completed in 1734, is depicted here as it originally looked. Rebuilt in 1745, that incarnation of the building still stands today, the oldest structure not only in New Orleans but in the entire Louisiana Purchase territory.

The Government House, the French and Spanish capitol building, was built in 1761 on Decatur at Toulouse Street, and remained in use as the American capital of Louisiana until it burned in 1828.

Built in 1788, the house known as Madame John's Legacy at 632 Dumaine Street is probably the second oldest standing building in the French Quarter. It is a rare and important example of Spanish Colonial architecture in New Orleans.

A slightly newer building from the same period is the Duroche-Castillon House, commonly called Lafitte's Blacksmith Shop at 941 Bourbon, built about 1790. Rumored links with the Pirate Jean Lafitte are without historical evidence but the house is a fascinating and important structure nonetheless.

The Orue-Pontalba House, completed in 1796 at the corner of Chartres and St. Peter Streets, is the subject an 1890 image by the New Orleans photographer Mugnier. The house's exterior appearance is still much the same though it was extensively rebuilt in 1962 as part of the Petit Theatre de Vieux Carre.

This 19th-century engraving of Dauphine Street shows the area as it appeared during the Spanish Colonial era. A drainage canal once ran down its center.

The Place d'Armes, also known as the Plaza de Armas and Jackson Square, was laid out as the parade ground for the military defending the Louisiana colony. The parish church of St. Louis stood where the Basilica of St. Louis, better known as St. Louis Cathedral, stands today. Military barracks once occupied either side of the square. It was here, on December 20, 1803, that the American flag was first raised above New Orleans.

The Place d'Armes was renamed Jackson Square in 1851 to honor Gen. Andrew Jackson, hero of the Battle of New Orleans. In January 1815, Andrew Jackson led the American troops in defense of the city, defending and saving it from an attack by the British in the final battle of the War of 1812. Neither side was aware at the time that hostilities had formally ended two weeks earlier. The following structures, from left to right, appear in the 1890s view above: the Cabildo, St. Louis Cathedral, the Presbytere, and the Lower Pontalba Building.

This view of the Cabildo, St. Louis Cathedral, and the statue of General Jackson is from around 1900. The statue, by sculptor Clark Mills, was erected in 1856. During the Union occupation in the Civil War, its base was defaced by Gen. Benjamin Butler with a misquote from Jackson: "The Union Must and Shall be Preserved." The cathedral appears here as it has since the present facade was constructed in 1849.

The Cabildo, situated to the left of the cathedral, was built in 1796 by the Spanish regime. It has served as the Louisiana Capitol Building, the New Orleans City Hall, the Louisiana State Supreme Court, and as a public library, fire station, prison, police court, and city notary's office. In 1911, it became part of the Louisiana State Museum. Here, on December 20, 1803, the formal transfer of Louisiana from France to the United States took place. The present mansard roof and cupola were added in 1847. The view at left is of the interior of the arched gallery that runs across the Cabildo's primary façade, looking out upon Jackson Square.

President William McKinley stands upon the balcony of the Cabildo with Mayor Paul Capdeville on May 2, 1901. McKinley is one of many heads of state to have visited the Cabildo. In 1825 the building was actually turned into an official residence for the Marquis de Lafayette during his stay in the city.

Pictured at right is the courtyard of the Cabildo. Doors along the galleries open to cells that once housed prisoners including, in 1814, the pirate Pierre Lafitte, brother of Jean Lafitte.

These two *c.* 1900 views show the stairs and massive wrought-iron gates of the Cabildo, which were fashioned in 1850 by the Pelanne Brothers of New Orleans. In 1988 fire swept through the building, causing extensive damage. Fortunately, most of the contents and important architectural elements, such as those shown here, were saved. In 1994 the thoroughly restored Cabildo was re-opened to the public.

In 1907, the Cabildo, the cathedral, and the Presbytere appeared very much as they do today. The Presbytere is a near-twin to the Cabildo, built in 1813 as an ecclesiastical structure associated with the cathedral next door. Like the Cabildo, the Presbytere is now part of the Louisiana State Museum. The cathedral was consecrated in 1794 and stands upon the site of earlier churches dating back to the city's founding. The present facade was designed by J.N.B. dePouilly in 1847. Construction on it began in 1849 and was completed three years later.

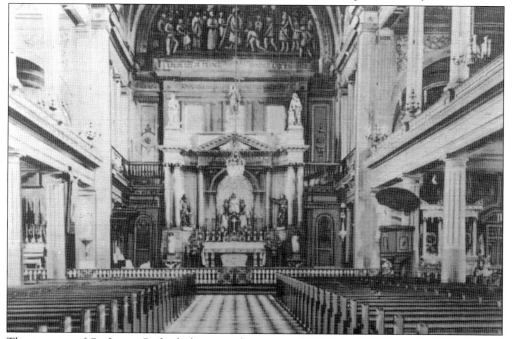

The interior of St. Louis Cathedral appears here around 1910. In 1964 Pope Paul VI elevated the cathedral to a minor basilica.

Behind the Cabildo, facing St. Peter Street, is the Arsenal, which has been a building of the Louisiana State Museum since 1914. Constructed in 1839, it was used by the Orleans artillery from 1846 to 1862. Until the capture of New Orleans in 1862, it served as Gen. P.G.T. Beauregard's headquarters; after the capture, it was used as a Federal prison. In 1874 it was occupied by the metropolitan police.

On either side of Jackson Square stand the twin Upper and Lower Pontalba Buildings, large red brick rowhouses with shops on their lower floors. Built by the Baroness Micaela de Pontalba in 1850, their ironwork displays the Baroness' family monogram: "A.P." for Almonester-Pontalba.

An 1890s photograph by G.F. Mugnier depicts the Pedesclaux-Lemonnier House, located on the corner of Royal and St. Peter Streets. Begun about 1795, it was unfinished as designed until 1811, when it was finally completed. It was, at the time, the tallest building (excepting church towers) in the city. Probably designed by architect Barthelemy Lafon, its apartments have been home to many prominent New Orleans citizens.

The French Market, appearing here in the late 19th century, began in 1791 on its present site. The oldest part of the present market is the end nearest Jackson Square, built in 1813 but subsequently remodeled many times. Originally the meat market, this section is now famous as the home to the Cafe du Monde coffee house. The vegetable market was added in 1823 and the entire complex was greatly enlarged in 1930. Once New Orleans boasted many such markets, though the French Market has always been the oldest and best known.

A praline vendor sets up shop near the market around 1920. By this date, such colorful figures that were once commonplace at the markets were beginning to vanish.

The Napoleon House at Chartres and St. Louis Streets, pictured here c. 1900, was built by Mayor Nicholas Girod as his residence in 1814. In 1832 Girod offered his home to Napoleon Bonaparte as part of a planned attempt to rescue the deposed and exiled emperor from St. Helena and bring him to New Orleans. Napoleon, however, died before the plan could be executed. The building has long been home to a famous bar and restaurant called the Napoleon House.

The Paul Morphy House, located at 417 Royal Street and shown here c. 1900, now houses Brennan's, one of the city's famous restaurants. Morphy, a world famous chess champion, built the structure to house a bank around 1800.

One of the Vieux Carre's most remarkable residential structures is the Gardette-LePretre House, located at 716 Dauphine Street. Built in 1836, the house's extraordinary cast-iron galleries were added several years later. It is commonly, but erroneously, believed that the ironwork of New Orleans dates from the French or Spanish eras, yet almost all that can be seen today is from the American period.

This building is located at 436 Chartres, across St. Louis Street from the Napoleon House. Dating from the early years of the American period, it once housed a slave dealer's offices and later a grocery. Today it is a bar.

The Lalurie House at 1140 Royal
Street is also known as "The Haunted
House." Built in the early years of the
19th century, it was attacked and badly
damaged in 1834 by a mob angered at
disclosures of cruelty to slaves there.
George Washington Cable, the noted
New Orleans writer of the late 19th
century, immortalized the event in his
book, *Strange True Stories of Louisiana*.
The upper photograph shows the
house as seen from Gov. Nicholls
Street (formerly Hospital Street). The
photograph at right shows the main
doorway of the house today.

This 19th-century view of the Convent of the Sisters of the Holy Family shows its louvered balcony, which provided privacy for the nuns. Located at 717 Orleans Street, the convent is now a hotel. Prior to its use as a convent, the building housed the famous Salle d'Orleans or Quadroon Ballroom, where young white men attended weekly dances for the purpose of acquiring quadroon mistresses. Such balls were held regularly in the city from 1790 until the Civil War.

This c. 1920 view of the corner of Royal and Dumaine Streets shows two early-19th-century structures. The house pictured to the far left was built in about 1805. The house at right, built in 1833, is known as "Tite Poulette's Dwelling," after a story by G.W. Cable.

A 19th-century security measure consisted of curved spikes of wrought iron set atop garden walls to prevent them from being scaled by intruders. This example is found on Governor Nicholls Street. Similarly menacing spikes and bladed devices of iron can be found between the levels of balconies on many French Quarter houses, effectively preventing potential intruders from climbing the supporting posts and reaching the galleries above.

Early-19th-century New Orleans houses were typically built around a central courtyard that doubled as a service area and garden. The courtyard pictured here in about 1910 belongs to the house at 913 Royal Street.

These early-20th-century views show two different early-19th-century courtyards. Pictured at left is the Court of the Two Sisters on Royal Street. Below is the Patio Royal, also on Royal Street. Both still exist and are typical of French Quarter houses from the era, most of which are still private homes and rarely seen by the eyes of the public

This early-20th-century view shows the courtyard of the Cabildo as it appeared around 1905. The similarity between the courtyards of private and public buildings is strikingly depicted here.

This photograph of the stairway of the Lyle Saxon residence on Royal Street was taken around 1920. Saxon was a pioneer and driving force behind the preservation of the Vieux Carre. The house shown here, one of several he restored and lived in, was a home-away-from-home for many of the nation's important artists and writers of the era.

This striking soft-focus image of a young lady in c. 1800 fashion, produced around 1920 by Moses Studios of New Orleans, is entitled "In a Garden of Yesteryear." Its original caption reads: "Recalling a time when mademoiselle wore crinolines and when her days were spent within the family walls. In the seclusion of the courtyard the ladies enjoyed their ices on balmy afternoons and gossiped to their hearts' content."

These French Quarter rooftops are located in the vicinity of Chartres and Barracks Streets looking toward Esplanade. The bottom photograph provides a peek into a lush garden courtyard behind a house facing Barracks Street.

31

The variety of styles, sizes, and functions of residential structures of the French Quarter is clearly visible in this view of Chartres Street looking from Barracks Street to Esplanade. Only when viewed from above or within can the full range of French Quarter architectural types be fully appreciated. From the street, each block appears as an unbroken procession of buildings, their facades flush with the sidewalk and offering little, if any, glimpse of what lies beyond.

The Le Carpentier-Beauregard-Keyes House, located at 1113 Chartres Street (a block from the scene at the top of the page), was built in 1826. After the Civil War, the house was the residence of Confederate Gen. P.G.T. Beauregard. Later it was the home of writer Francis Parkinson Keyes. The large building to the left of the house in this 1930s photograph has since been demolished and replaced by a lovely garden.

This view of Chartres Street was produced during the Federal occupation of New Orleans during the Civil War. With his back to Canal Street, the photographer looks toward the cathedral in the distance. Many of the buildings shown still stand today. Although the image was made in the early 1860s, it provides a good impression of how the French Quarter looked during the antebellum era.

The two French Quarter houses on this page were built in styles favored in the 19th century. The Federal-style house pictured at left was built around mid-century at 840 Conti. Below, the house at 918 Ursulines is a typical double cottage dating from late in the century, though similar to much earlier houses commonly found in the Quarter. Both houses on this page were home to the noted New Orleans photographer Ernest J. Bellocq, who is especially famous for his "Storyville Portraits" taken in the city's red light district around 1912–13. Bellocq resided at the Conti Street building at the time the Storyville images were produced. He lived in the Ursulines Street house at the time of his death in 1949.

Both of the alleys pictured in these early-20th-century views flank St. Louis Cathedral. Above is Pere Antoine Alley, originally named North Orleans Street but changed around 1900 to honor Father Antonio de Sedella, the beloved priest better known as Pere Antoine. He is buried inside the cathedral, the rear garden of which is enclosed by the fence at right. Pirate's Alley, originally South Orleans Street, is shown in the photograph at right. It was named in commemoration of Dominic You and the brothers Pierre and Jean Lafitte, legendary pirates who influenced early-19th-century New Orleans history.

Orleans Street, as laid out by Pauger, ended abruptly at the rear wall of the cathedral. In 1831 the street was stopped at Royal and the remaining space turned into a garden. This engraving from *Harper's Weekly* dates from 1861 and shows the rear of the cathedral seen from several blocks down Orleans Street.

Looking up Madison Street from Decatur Street, *c.* 1895, one can see Begue's Restaurant, one of the city's best known and popular eating places from 1856 to early in the 20th century. It successor, Tujague's, now occupies the same location with little change to the place's atmosphere.

Galatoire's Restaurant, located at 209 Bourbon Street, was established by Jean Galatoire, a native of Pau, France. Jean came to New Orleans in the 1890s, opening a small cafe on Dauphine Street. A few years later he purchased Victor's, one of the city's finest restaurants of the day, from its founder and Jean's close friend, Victor Bero, who had established it in the 1860s. People gradually began calling Victor's "Galatoire's," and in 1905 the name was formally changed. Little else has changed at Galatoire's over the years, however, and the restaurant remains one of the finest and most respected in the city.

Perhaps the most famous of all New Orleans restaurants is Antoine's, founded in 1840. The restaurant has hosted countless celebrities, including royalty (both actual royalty and, traditionally, Mardi Gras royalty as well), heads of state, and, it is said, every president of the United States since its founding by Antoine Alciatore (though not all were in office when they dined here). The restaurant has been in its present location at 713 St. Louis Street since 1868. It was here that Oysters Rockefeller was created in 1899 by Jules Alciatore, one of Antoine's 18 children. The wine cellar is one of the nation's finest, with some 23,000 bottles of standing stock, some over a century old.

The St. Louis Hotel on St. Louis Street, between Chartres and Royal Streets, was one of the grandest hotels in America when it was built in 1836. Heavily damaged by fire in 1841, the hotel was immediately rebuilt to the same design by architect J.N.B. dePouilly. The St. Louis, also known simply as "The Exchange," contained several restaurants, shops, interior access to a major bank, and a spectacular rotunda (below) in which auctions of all sorts were held, including art, real estate, and slaves.

The rotunda's dome, rising 88 feet above the floor, contained frescoes by the painter Domenico Canova (later salvaged and now in Paris). When this photo was taken around 1900, the upper level of the rotunda had been floored.

During Reconstruction, the grand St. Louis Hotel was used as the state capitol building, and the upper levels of the once-grand rotunda were floored to create chambers for the senate and legislature. These renovations were not removed after the seat of government was moved to Baton Rouge in 1882. In 1881 Gov. Louis A. Wiltz laid in state in the senate chamber.

On a level far below, the original auction block remained where it had been before the Civil War. This image was taken in the 1890s.

In its final incarnation, the St. Louis Hotel became the Hotel Royal, although it never regained its antebellum splendor. Too many alterations and advancing deterioration too costly to repair sealed its fate, and in 1903 the hotel was closed for good. These views were made in 1905 (above) and 1907 (below). In 1915 it was damaged by a violent hurricane, and in 1917 the hotel, which could accommodate 600 guests and boasted a bar once described as being "only a little smaller than the main reading room of the British Museum," was demolished.

For many years the location of the St. Louis Hotel was occupied by a parking lot. In 1957 plans for a new hotel to occupy the same site were drawn by Richard Koch and Sam Wilson Jr. and a few years later the present Omni Royal Orleans Hotel was built on the site. Roughly approximating the exterior appearance of its predecessor (but without the famous dome), the Royal Orleans actually incorporates part of a wall of the old St. Louis Hotel, seen here along its Chartres Street side.

Architect J.N.B. dePouilly's original plan for the St. Louis Hotel called for the creation of a new street running between and parallel to Royal and Chartres Streets. This street was known as Exchange Passage and ran from Canal Street through four city blocks to the front entrance of the hotel. Ultimately, the passage became a sort of open-air shopping arcade. In 1901 the passage's route was shortened when the block fronting the hotel was levelled to build the Civil District Court House, now the State Supreme Court, but long known as the Wildlife and Fisheries Building.

Behind the St. Louis Hotel, on Toulouse Street, stood the once-splendid building of the Citizens' Bank of Louisiana, also designed by dePouilly and featuring frescoed ceilings by Canova. Built in 1836, it was connected directly to the hotel by an interior entrance to the rotunda. Ruined by the Civil War, the bank failed and its headquarters sat vacant for almost 30 years before it was demolished. It is seen here about 1890 in its last days. Before the war, the Citizens' Bank issued $10 notes printed in English and French with the French word *Dix* (ten) prominently displayed. The notes came to be called "Dixies," a name later applied to the entire region in which they circulated: Dixie.

Another great antebellum bank was the Louisiana State Bank, the main building of which, seen here about 1910, still stands at the corner of Royal and Conti Streets. Built in 1820, it was designed by Benjamin H.B. Latrobe, also the architect of the U.S. Capitol Building in Washington D.C. Latrobe died of yellow fever in 1820 and is buried in St. Louis Cemetery Number One on Basin Street.

One of the best-known Vieux Carre landmarks of the late 19th century was the French Opera House, designed by James Gallier and built in 1859 at the corner of Bourbon and Toulouse Streets. It seated 1,600 and boasted four galleries above the main floor. Virtually all of the world's greatest opera stars, actors, actresses, and musicians of the late 19th and early 20th centuries performed on its stage at some point during its 60 seasons.

All came to an end, however, when the French Opera House burned down on December 4, 1919, 60 years and 2 days after its opening. A hotel occupies the site today.

This view of the sweeping crescent of the Mississippi River looking over the French Quarter was taken about 1910. The Civil District Courts Building is prominently visible at the center with the St. Louis Hotel and its dome just to the left. Behind the St. Louis one can barely see the rooftops of the Pontalba Buildings, a smokestack rising almost between them in the image. The tall building at far right is the Monteleone Hotel, a Royal Street landmark built in 1908. City planners at the time encouraged the demolition of French Quarter buildings, hoping they would make way for the growth of a modern urban center in their place. Fortunately, the majority of the quarter's old landmarks survived, and today form the nucleus of the city's universal appeal. Nevertheless, much has been lost through demolition, development, and deterioration. Even today, the French Quarter, the heart and soul of New Orleans, is still not out of danger.

Two

CANAL STREET

Canal Street is the principal thoroughfare of central New Orleans. Between the river and Basin Street, it divides the Vieux Carre from the Central Business District. Above Basin it forms the main corridor through Mid-City New Orleans. In the 19th century, Canal Street was the dividing line between the geographic centers of New Orleans' two dominant and often conflicting cultures: the Latin and Anglo Saxon. Its median came to be known as the "neutral ground" since it lay in neither camp. Although much of Canal Street's neutral ground has been replaced by bus and streetcar lanes, the term is still used in Louisiana to denote a boulevard median. For the record, there was never a canal where Canal Street now runs; one was planned in the early 19th century, but for multiple reasons was never built. The view above dates from about 1890.

In April 1862, Union forces captured New Orleans, the most important city of the Confederacy both in size and economics. When Capt. Theodorus Bailey and Lieut. George H. Perkins entered the city to demand its surrender, their reception was less than hospitable, as seen in this contemporary engraving. The scene is Canal Street as the men walk up from the river where the Federal fleet is anchored. A crowd follows jeering and taunting.

Designed by Alexander T. Wood, construction on the Customhouse on Canal at Decatur began in 1848 and continued to the time of the Civil War, at which time it was abruptly halted and left uncompleted until 1875. During its life it has served as the main post office, Federal Building, and as a Union prison after the Civil War. In September 1874, the block of Canal Street in front of the building was the scene of a fierce battle between pro- and anti-Reconstruction elements vying for power in post-Civil War Louisiana government.

On September 14, 1874, Canal Street between St. Charles Street and Royal Street was the scene of a mass demonstration that turned into an attempted coup against the Reconstruction government of Gov. William Pitt Kellogg, who was almost universally condemned as corrupt and unfit to serve. Five thousand men attended the rally at the base of the Henry Clay Monument, which then stood on the neutral ground. They then went home, gathered arms, and returned to confront the Metropolitan Police, which constituted a sort of private army for Kellogg. The event became known as the Battle of Liberty Place. The Liberty Monument later erected nearby has become a point of controversy in the late 20th century. It was moved in the 1990s to an obscure location near the Aquarium of the Americas. The Henry Clay statue, unveiled in 1860, was moved to Lafayette Square in 1901.

al Street after Snow-Storm of 1895.
New Orleans, La.

Electric streetcars appear on Canal Street after a rare snowstorm in 1895. Beginning in 1832, horse-drawn omnibusses were the first means of public transportation in New Orleans. Street railways began that same decade with cars pulled by mules and horses. In the 1880s a few cars were fitted with steam engines, yet it was the advent of electric streetcars in 1893 that finally eliminated the need for literal "horse-power." New Orleans was the second city in Louisiana to employ electric streetcars as public transportation (Shreveport was first, three years earlier). By 1964 the streetcars had been replaced by busses on Canal and virtually all other New Orleans streets. Only the St. Charles-Carrollton line remained in operation. In 1998, however, it was announced that streetcars would soon be returning to Canal Street.

The Mercier Building, located at Canal and Dauphine Streets, was built in 1887 on the former site of the Christ Episcopal Church, which was built in 1847. Its principal tenant was the A. Shwartz & Sons Dry Goods Company. In 1897 Shwartz & Sons changed its name to the Maison Blanche Department Store, who demolished the building and the old Grand Opera House next door in 1909 in order to build the Maison Blanche Building. It was remodelled to house the Ritz-Carlton Hotel in 1999.

The Maison Blanche Building dominates this view of Canal Street, c. 1920. Canal Street, then the city's busiest shopping area, was lined with department stores, haberdasheries, millineries, jewellers, specialty stores of all kinds, and numerous office buildings, especially on the uptown side.

Mardi Gras and New Orleans are virtually synonymous in many minds. Canal Street has always been the main thoroughfare of Mardi Gras, though its parades and revelry spread throughout the city. Mardi Gras balls began around the 1820s and parades by 1837. By the 1850s the festivities had grown huge and private krewes had begun to form, each putting on their own balls and parades. Rex, King of Carnival, was born in 1872 and has been of central importance to Mardi Gras ever since. "Throws," beads and baubles thrown from passing floats, are an old tradition, but the well-known "doubloons" of Mardi Gras are a relatively recent addition to the festivities. This Mardi Gras parade took place on Canal Street around 1905.

The Comus parade of 1867 took place on St. Charles Street in the Central Business District, having passed in from Canal Street. Post-Civil War Mardi Gras celebrations were especially festive as the carnival was not held during the Federal occupation of the city from 1862 to 1866.

In this view of a parade on Canal Street in the 1910s, one can see an unofficial Mardi Gras flag flying at far left. Although this flag is common at Mardi Gras, the official flag has stripes running diagonally, rather than horizontally. The colors of the flag—and of Mardi Gras—are purple, gold, and green.

During this Mardi Gras parade on Canal Street in the 1910s, thousands of spectators, virtually all in suits and hats, lined the streets in a seemingly orderly fashion. Today Mardi Gras is far from orderly and the throngs of spectators are even larger. Nor were celebrants necessarily better behaved in past times. Frequent comments appeared in the 19th-century press that revelers too often behaved in a vulgar and promiscuous manner. Today the success of a particular year's carnival is often measured in terms of the amount of litter left behind when the party ends.

This World War I view of Canal Street faces away from the river. A sign advertising the Orpheum Theatre hung above the intersection of St. Charles and Canal where the Henry Clay statue had stood before. It was illuminated at night by hundreds of electric light bulbs. Formerly the St. Charles Theatre, the Orpheum was located on St. Charles Street just off Canal, a short distance outside the photograph's left-hand margin.

This photograph of the French Quarter side of Canal Street was taken in 1901, when the population of New Orleans was 290,000. At the corner of Royal Street, one can see the Marx Brothers clothing store, and three buildings to the left is the Bourbon Street intersection. The streetcar at left is bound for Jackson Avenue in the Garden District.

Lined with stores, theaters, and hotels, and filled with streetcars, automobiles, and pedestrians, Canal Street was, and is, unquestionably New Orleans' "Main Street." This late 1920s view shows the street looking from the river toward the lake. In 1930 Canal underwent a massive repaving and beautification program in which ornamental street lamp standards were installed, each with the insignia of the nations which have dominated New Orleans—France, Spain, the Confederate States, and the United States—on their bases. Some of these can still be seen today, as can the brass street signs embedded into the sidewalks at intersections at the same time. The city's population at this time was over 450,000.

The tall buildings of the Central Business District can be seen to the left in this view of Canal Street in the early 1930s. At far right is the edge of the French Quarter. The image is from the 600 block looking west.

The Southern Railway Terminal at Canal and Basin Streets opened in 1908, and is pictured here about 1940 looking from Elk Place. After World War II the Veterans' Service Center Building occupied the site of this park, but it was later removed and the park restored. Today a string of monuments line the neutral ground of Basin Street where the terminal, demolished in 1954, once stood.

St. Charles Street is shown here looking into the American Sector, today's Central Business District, from Canal Street, about 1870. In the distance is the St. Charles Hotel, the only competitor to the St. Louis Hotel for the distinction of being the city's grandest. The St. Charles, designed by James Gallier and built in 1842, burned in 1851 but was rebuilt with the exception of its original tall dome. The second incarnation of the hotel, pictured here, stood until 1894 when it, too, was destroyed by fire. A third St. Charles, of entirely different design, opened in 1896 and was demolished in 1974. A high-rise office structure now occupies the site. The building at right still stands, though much altered. The building behind it with the cast-iron galleries housed Kolb's Restaurant, famous for decades for both its Creole and German dishes. The streetcars shown were horse-drawn.

Three

THE CENTRAL
BUSINESS DISTRICT

The skyline of the Central Business District dominates the horizon in this modern photograph shot from the roof of the Garden District's Pontchartrain Hotel. The "CBD," as the district is commonly known, is the center of business and commerce for the Crescent City. The great buildings of the modern city stand upon the site of the former American Sector, the Anglo-Saxon parallel to the French Quarter. Much of the old American Sector has vanished, but many grand 19th- and early-20th-century buildings remain nestled among their late-20th-century counterparts here. The mammoth Superdome is visible to the far left in the image.

The St. Charles Hotel was in ruins on April 30, 1894, the day after a fire destroyed it. At its height the hotel could accommodate 700 guests at a time. After the Civil War, its owners provided free accommodations to returning Confederate soldiers. The dining room was universally renowned, said to be ranked alongside the finest restaurants of Paris in every respect.

The old Touro Synagogue, completed in 1857 at 836 Carondelet Street, was once home to the oldest Jewish congregation established outside the original 13 colonies. Founded in 1827 and named for philanthropist Judah Touro, who richly endowed the congregation, the synagogue constructed its present St. Charles Avenue location in 1904. In 1907 the old synagogue became the Knights of Columbus Hall; it was demolished in the 1940s.

A fixture on Poydras Street, Maylie's Restaurant was a longtime CBD landmark. Founded in 1876, it had recently closed when this photograph was made in 1990. Remodeled in 1998, it now houses part of the Smith & Wollensky steakhouse. Originally, the once-bustling Poydras Market stood opposite Maylie's where the street's neutral ground lies today. A few blocks toward the river is another Poydras Street landmark, Mother's Restaurant, which is still in operation.

Located in the center of the CBD, Lafayette Square is the second oldest public square in New Orleans. Laid out in 1796, it did not receive its present name until the 19th century. In this 1902 photograph is the monument to philanthropist John McDonogh, placed in the square in 1898. When he died in 1850, McDonogh left a substantial portion of his estate to establish a public school system in New Orleans. For his generosity, many local schools are named for him. To the left is the Henry Clay statue, moved from Canal Street in 1901. The old public library and the Lafayette Hotel appear in the background.

The U.S. Fifth Circuit Court of Appeals, formerly the main post office, occupies the site of the library and hotel today. It has changed little since the 1930s, when this photograph was taken.

The Hibernia National Bank Building, completed in 1925, dominates this view looking up Carondelet Street from Canal Street in 1926. Its columned cupola towering above made it the city's tallest building at the time, although it has long since been dwarfed by its surroundings. To the left, with the pyramidal corner roof, is the Liverpool, London, & Globe Building, destined to stand only a few months after this image was made.

The grandiose lobby of the Hibernia National Bank Building has changed little since this photo was taken in the late 1920s. The lobby area covers a half-acre of space and is finished in Tavernelle marble and American walnut. The fittings are all of bronze.

A short distance away, on Baronne Street, is the Moorish-style Church of the Immaculate Conception, originally built in 1851 and rebuilt due to structural weakness in 1928.

A short walk from Gallier Hall stands the Scottish Rite Temple, built in 1851 at 619 Carondelet Street as the Carondelet Street Methodist Church. It originally boasted a cupola patterned after the Ancient Greek Tower of the Winds (at right). Unfortunately the cupola has long since been lost and the main entrance has been somewhat reconfigured, although the building still stands and remains an important example of Greek Revival architecture in the CBD. The building is shown below as it appears today.

Another important Greek Revival building and a centerpiece of the CBD is the old city hall, built in 1845 and now known as Gallier Hall. Facing Lafayette Square, Gallier Hall was designed by the prominent New Orleans architect James Gallier Sr., for whom it is named. The building served as the seat of city government for nearly 12 decades. Additionally, the bodies of Gov. Isaac Johnson, Confederate president Jefferson Davis, Gen. P.G.T. Beauregard, Chief of Police David Hennessy, Bertie Sneed (the first casualty of the Spanish-American War), and Mayors Martin Behrman and deLesseps S. "Chep" Morrison have all lain in state here. After the surrender of the city in 1862, the building was seized by Federal forces (below).

A crowd gathered in the 200 block of Girod Street (above) on October 16, 1890, due to events from the previous night. At age 32, Police Chief David C. Hennessey (pictured at right) was gunned down by members of the Sicilian Mafia, making him the first prominent public official in any American city to be assassinated by the Mafia. Hennessey had actively investigated the Mafia presence in New Orleans and his murder came as he was on his way home from a meeting of the police board at city hall. Nineteen suspects were arrested, tried, and ultimately acquitted of plotting and carrying out the assassination. On March 14, 1891, a mob of outraged citizens attacked the Parish Prison where the former suspects were about to be released, lynching 11 of them. Hennessey was buried with honors at Metairie Cemetery.

Built in 1883, the New Orleans Cotton Exchange stood on the corner of Carondelet and Gravier Streets until the 1920s. One of several cotton exchange buildings in New Orleans, this was by far the most impressive and elaborately detailed. Here Southern cotton was sold to Northern and European textile manufacturers. Cotton traders, factors, buyers, and brokers could be found on the floor along with steamboat captains, planters, speculators, and a host of others. The Cotton Exchange and Sugar Exchange were to 19th-century New Orleans what Wall Street has been to 20th-century New York. This photo was taken in about 1905. The Cotton Exchange closed in 1964.

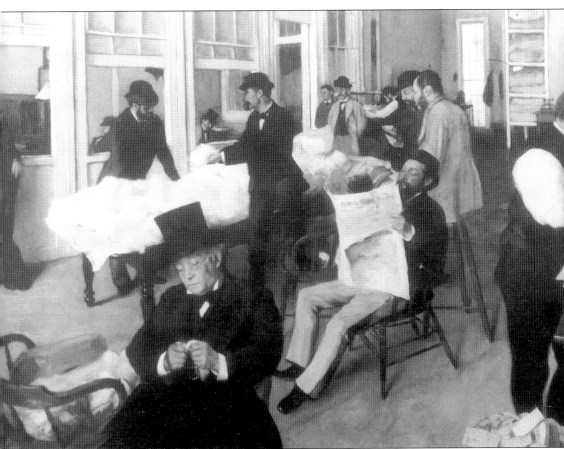

The Cotton Market, New Orleans, painted by Edgar Degas at the time of his brief residence in the city (1872–73), depicts a scene inside the Musson cotton office on Carondelet Street. Degas stayed in the city with his mother's relatives, the Musson family, in their home at 2308 Esplanade (still standing though much altered). Reproduced by the kind permission of the Museum of Fine Arts, Pau, France, the painting features Degas' brothers, Achille and Rene, both New Orleans cotton merchants. Rene (center) is reading the newspaper, while Achille (far left) leans against a partition opening. Degas' uncle, Michel Musson, formerly postmaster of New Orleans, examines a sample of cotton in the foreground. Pictured in the center is a cotton grading table, which brokers used to examine cotton.

"Big Charity," as New Orleans' huge Charity Hospital is known, is one of the major public medical centers of the nation. Located on the edge of the CBD, it faces Claiborne Avenue, Tulane Avenue, and Interstate 10, separating the CBD from Mid-City New Orleans. The Tulane University School of Medicine is included in the Charity Hospital complex, which has grown markedly in size since this aerial photograph was made in 1965. Tulane Avenue runs diagonally across the lower right-hand portion of the image.

Four

THE RIVER
AND THE PORT

It is no exaggeration to say that the Mississippi is and has always been the lifeblood of the city of New Orleans. The port made it one of the great North American cities and one of the nation's largest during the 19th century. Even today the port of New Orleans is the fourth busiest in the United States in terms of total tonnage handled annually. After the American takeover of New Orleans in 1803, the city mushroomed in size and importance almost overnight. Hardly more than a village in 1803, New Orleans had almost 30,000 people by 1820; over 100,000 by 1840; and by the time of the Civil War, its population was approaching 170,000. The city's importance grew as more and more settlers began to populate the Midwest and West, of which the principal trade and travel routes were the Mississippi and her tributaries. Above is a view of the New Orleans waterfront about 1850.

These two views of the wharf were taken at the foot of Bienville Street in about 1870. In the top image eight packet steamboats line up dockside. The one at right is a Red River packet boat, carrying mail, passengers, and commodities on a regular route from New Orleans up the Mississippi to the Red River, and thence up the Red to Shreveport and points between before making the trip back. The second from right is an Ouachita packet boat, which made similar runs but with Monroe, Louisiana, at the opposite end of the journey. Ocean-going vessels such as the masted steamer in the image below were seen in the 19th century less frequently than today.

An 1883 engraving from *Frank Leslie's Illustrated News* shows some three dozen steamboats lined up at the New Orleans levee. Carrying much more than mail and passengers, their principal cargoes consisted of massive quantities of sugar, cotton, grains, groceries, and consumer goods of every imaginable sort. The levee was a busy spot virtually 24 hours a day, filled with steamboat crewmen, dockworkers, sailors, peddlers, food vendors, and an array of others. Beggars, loafers, and prostitutes were never far away either, and for a time Gallatin Street, near the riverfront in the French Quarter, was considered the roughest place on earth. Some sense of the level of more legitimate wharf activity can be gained from this image, made at the time when cotton was truly the king of commodities.

Contrary to popular misconception, the golden age of cotton production in the South came after, not before, the Civil War. Many post-war steamers were fitted out to carry enormous amounts of baled cotton. The largest cotton cargo ever carried on any riverboat was the load shown here, which came to New Orleans aboard the *Henry Frank* on April 2, 1881, containing 9,226 bales.

This wharf view was captured 20 years later showing cotton bales waiting to be loaded aboard an ocean-going vessel bound for Europe.

The *Imperial*, photographed while docked at the foot of Canal Street on March 28, 1895, had carried 3,611 bales of cotton from Shreveport, the center of the state's cotton growing region. Like all cotton brought to New Orleans, this was intended for export to Northern or European textile mills. The *Imperial* met an odd fate: while in New Orleans for repairs in 1912, shrimp consumed the bottom of her hull and caused her to sink.

The *Era No. 10*, one of the great Mississippi-Red River packets, appears here loaded with cotton in the 1870s. She burned in 1892. Because it was flammable and also heavy if waterlogged, cotton was a dangerous cargo to carry in massive quantities, and many cotton vessels either burned or sank. Its value made it worth the risks, however.

The *America* docks at the foot of Canal Street while her cargo of cotton is unloaded around 1900. Built in 1898, the *America* operated principally on the Mississippi and Ouachita Rivers during her distinguished 28-year career. She mainly carried cotton, but also transported such varied commodities as gunpowder, beer, soap, and even automobiles. In 1924 she was used in the making of a silent movie entitled *Magnolia*, years before New Orleans became the popular movie-making venue it is today.

The *Kate Wood*, steaming to New Orleans, was loaded to her uppermost deck with North Louisiana cotton, *c.* 1890. This was once a common scene on the Mississippi at New Orleans.

This pre-Civil War view of the New Orleans levee was made in 1859 by "Edwards, Photographer." Three of the boats shown are Red River packets, two are Ouachita River packets, and one is a Yazoo River packet. Hundreds of such boats traveled into and out of New Orleans annually both before and after the war. The cotton in the foreground has been unloaded from these boats and represents the produce of plantations in Northwest Louisiana, Northeast Louisiana, and Mississippi.

This view shows the same site 36 years later. Sugar is the cargo being handled here.

The *Robt. E. Lee* offloads cotton at New Orleans in about 1870. That same year, the *Robt. E. Lee* had its famous race with the *Natchez* on the Mississippi River. The size and splendor of many post-Civil War sidewheel steamboats is evidenced by such craft as the *Robt. E. Lee*, the *Robt. E. Lee II*, the *Richmond*, the *Natchez*, the *Belle Memphis*, and others of this class, all of which were frequently spotted at New Orleans.

A Mugnier photograph from the 1890s depicts the levee near Jackson Square. The boat is the Ouachita packet *D'Arbonne*.

The *Keokuk*, shown here offloading sugar while docked at the foot of Conti Street *c.* 1890, ran a weekly route between New Orleans, Donaldsonville, and Baton Rouge, the heart of South Louisiana sugar country. The spires of St. Louis Cathedral are visible behind the boat's foremast, and to the cathedral's left, the large brick structure is the Jackson Brewery, still standing, though markedly remodeled into a shopping mall. The upper floors of the Lower Pontalba Building on Jackson Square appear at far right. An ocean-going steamer is visible just behind the *Keokuk* and right below the Pontalba Building.

Besides cotton and sugar, New Orleans has been an important market for many other commodities, particularly coffee and bananas. The bulk of South American-grown coffee sold in the United States has passed through the port of New Orleans. The same is true for bananas, the trade of which began just after the Civil War. In this scene, bunches of bananas are unloaded by steam conveyor in 1900.

Dock workers strike near the foot of Canal Street around 1930. New Orleans was the scene of considerable labor unrest at its port early in the 20th century and much progress for wharf workers and longshoremen nationally was achieved here.

Five

STORYVILLE AND TREME

As New Orleans is famous as the birthplace of jazz, it has often been said that Storyville, the old red light district of New Orleans, was the specific origin of this musical genre. While there is considerable evidence that jazz was not necessarily born in Storyville, it certainly came of age there. Small bands played in the saloons and cafes of the district, while pianists could be found in several of the larger bordellos. In its earliest days jazz was not viewed as a particularly wholesome sort of music, but as time went by it came to be first tolerated, then accepted, later seen as mainstream, and finally celebrated. "Jazzfest," New Orleans' annual Jazz and Heritage Festival, is one of the nation's largest annual music festivals today. Thousands of tourists visit the Crescent City each year to indulge in the enjoyment of its world-famous jazz and blues offerings. This jazz band poses at Tom Anderson's Saloon on Basin Street in the early 20th century.

Tom Anderson's saloon, pictured here *c.* 1900, was located on the corner of Basin and Iberville Streets. The cupolas belong to "The Arlington" and its neighbor, "Mahogany Hall," the two largest Storyville brothels. Storyville, the city's legally established red light district, was opened in 1898 as a means of corralling the city-wide problem of prostitution into one restricted area. Within this new district prostitution was decriminalized and tolerated. At its height some 2,000 registered prostitutes plied their trade in Storyville, which also contained dozens of supporting businesses ranging from upscale establishments like Anderson's to seedy dives. Although neither the first nor the only such district in America, Storyville was certainly the best known, even publishing its own business directory, the Blue Book. The district covered a large area carved out of the Faubourg Treme and bounded by Basin, Iberville, and St. Louis Streets, and Claiborne Avenue. In 1917 the Storyville red light district was officially closed and prostitution again became illegal in New Orleans.

Few original Storyville structures survive today. After the district was closed by order of the federal government, banning the existence of such districts within 5 miles of a military installation, the prostitutes and madams scattered, leaving area buildings mostly vacant. Beginning in the early 1940s, the Iberville Housing Project began construction on the site of Storyville, and by 1949 virtually no trace of the old red light district remained. One of the few surviving buildings at the end of the 20th century is the old Joe Victor's Saloon on St. Louis at Villere Street, pictured above in 1943 and below in 1999.

Pictured above are two lone surviving Storyville buildings on Bienville at Crozat Streets in 1994. The one on the right, formerly Frank Early's Saloon, was the site where "Professor" Tony Jackson wrote the famous ragtime piano song "Pretty Baby." Ferdinand LeMenthe, better known as "Jelly Roll Morton," the district's other leading "professor," was also known to have played here. The building at left once housed several cheap one-girl "cribs," but has since been demolished. The scene below was taken by Walker Evans at Basin and Conti Streets. St. Louis Cemetery Number One is on the right, and May Tuckerman's bordello is on the left.

Madam May Tuckerman's bordello was typical of the Storyville brothels. Larger than the tiny "cribs" but smaller than the enormous bordellos operating up the street, Tuckerman's, located at 341 Basin, employed just a few girls at a time in this engaging little early-19th-century house, now demolished. Other earlier madams had held court there. In 1917, just before the district closed, Madam Willie Barrera took over the operation. Just behind this house stood that of Madam Gypsy Schaeffer, another center of early jazz.

Basin Street takes its name from the turning basin of the Carondelet Canal, which connected the town's then-outskirts to Bayou St. John, providing a waterway from the city to Lake Pontchartrain to its north. Built by Governor Carondelet in 1796, the canal was rebuilt and widened in 1805. The basin, later filled in, was located off Basin Street in the heart of Faubourg Treme, not far from St. Louis Cemetery Number One.

The Mortuary Chapel of St. Anthony on Rampart Street, located a block from St. Louis Cemetery Number One, was built in 1826 in order to move funerals away from the cathedral for fear of contagion. Rampart separates the Vieux Carre from Faubourg Treme. Much remodeled since this 1890 photograph, it is now the Church of Our Lady of Guadeloupe.

St. Louis Cemetery Number One, founded in 1789, was not the first cemetery in New Orleans, but is the oldest to survive. Originally located outside the city limits, the area around the cemetery was later developed by Claude Treme and came to be known as Faubourg Treme, or "Treme's Suburb." In this small block bounded by Basin, Conti, St. Louis, and Treme Streets, rest thousands of the city's early citizens, famous people and the common folk alike. The above-ground tombs are a noteworthy aspect of New Orleans cemeteries and have their roots in ancient Latin burial customs. Mayors, government officials from both the Colonial and American eras, victims of the Battle of New Orleans and the Civil War, as well as many others find their last rest here. Benjamin H.B. Latrobe, the architect of the U.S. Capitol, rests here as does the "Voodoo Queen" Marie Laveau. The most recent notable interment here was that of Mayor Ernest "Dutch" Morial in 1989.

St. Louis Cemetery Number Two is located a short distance away from St. Louis Number One. Bounded by Claiborne Avenue and Iberville, Robertson, and St. Louis Streets, it is trisected into three city squares by Bienville and Conti Streets, which pass through it. St. Louis Number Two was consecrated in 1823 after St. Louis Number One had grown too full. The image above was taken in 1900 or 1901, but the cemetery's general appearance has changed little since that time. As with its predecessor, St. Louis Number Two is filled with above-ground tombs containing the mortal remains of early New Orleanians from all walks of life.

For many years, the old Parish Prison on Orleans Avenue, pictured here c. 1890, was a Treme area landmark. Built upon part of the former de Morand Plantation between 1831 and 1836, the Parish Prison was demolished in 1895. In 1906 the City Pumping Station was constructed on its site.

Six

THE ESPLANADE RIDGE FROM MARIGNY TO THE LAKE

The Creole Faubourgs (suburbs) were the first neighborhoods of New Orleans to be developed outside the original city area, today's Vieux Carre. The first of the Faubourgs was laid out upon the site of the Bernard de Marigny plantation (above), hence its name: Faubourg Marigny. The plantation itself dated from the time of the city's founding, although the faubourg was established in 1805. The Marigny House was demolished about 1862. Dividing Marigny from the Vieux Carre is Esplanade Avenue, which runs all the way to Bayou St. John and the entrance to City Park.

The United States Branch Mint at 400 Esplanade was built in 1835 upon the site once occupied by Fort St. Charles, one of the city's defensive fortifications erected by the Spanish in 1792. Later the site was a public square called Jackson Square, not to be confused with the Jackson Square of today. The mint struck silver and gold coinage from 1838 to 1909. During the Civil War the bullion held there was seized by the state government. When the city was captured by Federal forces, a man named William Mumford ripped down the U.S. flag from the pole in front. He was subsequently hanged on the spot for this "crime." Following the war there was a hiatus of several years in the minting of new coins at New Orleans. In 1931 the building was briefly remodeled into a federal prison and then used by the Coast Guard; today it is part of the Louisiana State Museum system.

Only a few blocks down from the mint, this view of Esplanade Avenue in the 1890s shows the Vieux Carre on the left and Faubourg Marigny on the right. Streetcars run down the neutral ground at center. Some distance further toward Bayou St. John, along what is known as the Esplanade Ridge, many fine late-19th-century homes were constructed on what was essentially reclaimed swampland. Besides the French Quarter and Faubourg Marigny, Esplanade Avenue also runs through or near such historic neighborhoods as Faubourg Treme, New Marigny, Faubourg St. John, Faubourg Pontchartrain, and Parkview.

Gayarre Place, a small triangular "pocket park" at the juncture of Esplanade Avenue and Bayou Road, is the subject of this 1895 photograph by George F. Mugnier. Today the monument to noted 19th-century Louisiana historian Charles Etienne Gayarre still stands, though the sculpture on top has been replaced by a different one. The cast-iron fountain and owl sculpture have disappeared, however, as have the ducks who once resided there. The house at left in the background still stands facing Esplanade, but the cottage at right has long since been replaced by a large two-story frame house of the late Victorian period.

St. Roch Market, located in the New Marigny neighborhood, is still a thriving local market. The Faubourgs Nouvelle Marigny and Franklin form modern New Marigny, which borders the Gentilly area. These neighborhoods were once home to one of the nation's largest pre-Civil War free Black communities. Later, a large German population settled here as well.

The St. Roch Cemetery and its famous chapel, pictured here as they appeared in 1895, are located only a short distance from St. Roch Market. Jazz great "Jelly Roll Morton" once resided in the St. Roch area as did many other jazz musicians of the early 20th century.

The Jefferson Davis School was one of the many fine New Orleans school buildings of the late 19th and early 20th centuries, a period when the city was a leader in public education. Built in 1896 at 1932 Touro Street in New Marigny, it was indicative of schools constructed throughout the city at that time. Later it was the site of the Frederick Middle School. Many school names have been changed in recent years, stirring strong public emotions both pro and con in each instance.

The Old Spanish Custom House, a fine old home of the Spanish Colonial period, is believed to have been built in 1784 on the plantation of Don Santiago Lloreins. Today it faces Moss Street on the lower bank of Bayou St. John. Despite its popular name, there is no evidence the house was ever used as the Spanish Custom House. In the 20th century it was restored by Helen Pitkin Schertz, a local writer and newspaper columnist, and her husband, druggist Christian Schertz.

At the northernmost end of Esplanade Avenue, just below Bayou St. John, lies St. Louis Cemetery Number Three, chartered in 1856. Next to it are the fairgrounds, the sheds of which can be seen here just below the skyline of the Central Business District far off in the distance.

The grandiose Luling Mansion, shown here *c.* 1890, once faced Esplanade Avenue between Leda and Verna Streets, but in the 1920s the front, back, and side lawns were subdivided and houses were built there. Wings that once stood on either side of the house were demolished when the streets were built. The once-spacious grounds originally abutted St. Louis Cemetery Number Three and the Creole Racecourse, now the fairgrounds. The mansion was designed by the firm of Gallier and Esterbrook and completed in 1865. In 1871 it became home to the Louisiana Jockey Club. Again a private residence, it still stands at 1438 Leda Street.

The entrance to City Park is situated at the lake-end terminus of Esplanade Avenue. The park was established upon the site of the Allard Plantation, which was sold at a sheriff's sale to John McDonogh in 1845. McDonogh allowed Louis Allard to live there until his death in 1847 (he is buried in St. Louis Cemetery Number Two, not in the park as some say), and then donated the land to the city. In 1891 the park, as we know it today, was founded. The Isaac Delgado Museum, now the New Orleans Museum of Art, was later built in the park. This view is from 1913.

A Spanish defensive fortress, Fort San Juan, was built in 1769 at the mouth of Bayou St. John. In 1823 a resort known as Spanish Fort was laid out on the grounds nearby. In 1828 the site was expanded and in 1881 a casino added. Oscar Wilde lectured at the pavilion here, and numerous other notables of the 19th century stayed at the hotel or dined in its restaurants. The fort's ruins remain but the resort closed in 1928; its site is now occupied by a residential district.

Beyond City Park is West End, a pleasure resort on the shore of Lake Pontchartrain, opened in 1871 and pictured above *c.* 1895. West End boasted a hotel, pavilion, restaurant, and various amusement park structures, as well as a large over-the-water platform. A railway line took visitors directly to and from downtown New Orleans on open-sided cars. In 1896 the first motion picture ever seen in New Orleans debuted at West End. Today the site is occupied by West End Park, which opened in 1921.

The Southern Yacht Club is the second oldest yacht club in the nation. Founded at pass Christian, Mississippi, in 1849, the club moved to New Orleans after the Civil War. The clubhouse pictured was built in 1879 at West End. Although the old clubhouse is long gone, the yacht club is still located there, along with the municipal marina and the U.S. Coast Guard station at the north end of West End Boulevard at Lakeshore Drive.

A small submarine found in Lake Pontchartrain in 1879 was displayed at Spanish Fort in 1890 when this Mugnier image was made. In 1909 it was moved to the Confederate Veterans' Home, and now rests on the portico of the Presbytere on Jackson Square. It has been said that this is the Confederate sub *Pioneer*, although this is doubtful as evidence exists showing that the *Pioneer* was scrapped.

Boats such as these oyster luggers on Lake Pontchartrain brought in oysters from the lower coast of Louisiana, and could be seen on the levee of the Mississippi River and in the turning basin on Basin Street during the 19th century as well. Oysters have always been an important commodity in New Orleans. In addition to shrimp and crabs, they are among the staples of traditional New Orleanian cuisine. This photograph was taken *c.* 1890.

Seven

MID-CITY

Close to the hospital district that marks the boundary between the Central Business District and Mid-City, this house stands at 1565 Cleveland Street, on the corner with Robertson. Amazingly still standing amid parking lots and commercial sites, it was once the home of noted New Orleans writer Lafcadio Hearn, who came to New Orleans in 1877. While here, he wrote many wonderful, often bizarre and poignant, stories of the city and the surrounding region. Only George Washington Cable stands out as prominently among 19th-century New Orleans storytellers. Hearn later moved to Japan, where he is regarded as the foremost Western interpreter of Japanese culture. He died there in 1904. Hearn's onetime residence is typical of many that formerly stood in this part of Mid-City New Orleans, once known as "Back of Town." Not too far away to the northwest of Claiborne Avenue, the 20th-century part of Mid-City, once the heart of New Orleans, remains a vibrant neighborhood.

Charity Hospital on Tulane Avenue was built in 1832 and could house 500 patients at a time. The first Charity Hospital, built in 1739, was located on Rampart Street. Destroyed in the hurricane of 1779, it was rebuilt only to burn again in 1810. The third Charity Hospital opened on Canal Street in 1815, and in the 1830s it served as the state capitol building. The hospital pictured above stood until 1938, at which time it was demolished to build today's "Big Charity," as the mammoth hospital is known.

The Richardson Medical Building of Tulane Medical School stood on Canal Street between Robertson and Villere from 1893 to 1930. It is named for Dr. T.G. Richardson, a longtime early dean of the medical school.

The Jefferson Davis Memorial, dedicated February 22, 1911, stands on the neutral ground of the Jefferson Davis Parkway, facing Canal Street. Davis, president of the Confederate States of America from 1861 to 1865, died in New Orleans in 1889. He was initially interred at Metairie Cemetery, though later moved to Hollywood Cemetery in Richmond, Virginia. The monument's inscription reads, in part: "His name is enshrined in the hearts of the people for whom he suffered, and his deeds are forever wedded to immortality." Unfortunately, the monument and the name of the Jefferson Davis Parkway have become threatened by misguided "political correctness" and historical shortsightedness at the end of the 20th century.

The extraordinary home of tomb builder Charles A. Orleans is pictured here as it appeared at the time of its construction in 1889. Located at 1800 Canal Street, the house still stands as a Mid-City landmark, particularly outstanding among remaining houses of this area of town, despite the fact that much of the home's exuberant gingerbread ornamentation has been lost and its cupola modified. Since 1978 it has been home to the Orleans Parish Medical Society.

The old House of Detention, as the city jail was known in the late 19th century, stood on Tulane Avenue at Broad Street. Initially constructed as a hospital, it housed the jail for most of its career before being razed in the 1920s to make room for the present Criminal Courts Building.

The old Criminal Courts Building was built in 1893 at Tulane Avenue and Saratoga Street. Its site is today part of the location of the city hall complex, opened in 1957.

The area near the lake end of Canal Street is home to a remarkable cluster of historic cemeteries. Within a few blocks of the intersection of Canal Street and City Park Boulevard there are over a dozen burial grounds and at the intersection itself every corner is occupied by one. Above are the graves of Prayer Cemetery at Canal and Bottinelli Place, begun in 1846. It is the city's oldest extant Jewish cemetery. Gates from an earlier cemetery, dating from 1828, were moved here in 1957.

The African-American Holt Cemetery is located just off City Park Boulevard behind the Delgado Community College campus. It was opened in 1879. Many pioneers of jazz, blues, and ragtime music are buried here, some in unmarked graves.

At the intersection of City Park Boulevard and Canal Street, close to the point at which City Park Boulevard becomes Metairie Road, is Cypress Grove Cemetery. Sometimes called the Firemen's Cemetery because it was founded by a charitable organization of volunteer firefighters, Cypress Grove began in 1840. Many notable citizens rest here, and the cemetery is home to numerous important tombs and monuments of old New Orleans. The massive Egyptian Revival gates are visible in the background of the photograph, as are the Irad ferry tomb, first in the cemetery, marked by a broken column at left; the Perseverance Fire Company tomb, marked by the cupola at center; and the cast-iron Leeds tomb, at right. All date from the 1840s.

At the far lake end of Mid-City New Orleans is Metairie Cemetery. It is located within the city of New Orleans but it marks the boundary of the suburb of Metairie, today New Orleans' largest suburb. Founded in 1872 on the site of a former racecourse, the cemetery's older portion is laid out in the oval shape where the tracks once ran. Regarded as one of the most beautiful historic cemeteries in the United States, Metairie presents a parklike appearance despite its abundance of large above-ground tombs. Many of New Orleans' and Louisiana's most important personalities of the 19th and 20th centuries find their final rest here, including numerous mayors, governors, and civic, business, and religious leaders.

Eight

THE GARDEN DISTRICT
AND UPTOWN AREAS

The Lower Garden District and Garden District sections of New Orleans both predate the Civil War by several decades. In the 1820s several large plantations upstream from the then-city limits were developed into new faubourgs, such as Annunciation, Ste. Marie, Livaudais, de la Course, Solet, and others. In 1833 these were combined into a single suburb called the City of Lafayette. In 1852 the City of Lafayette (not to be confused with a modern south Louisiana city of that name, then called Vermillionville) was annexed to the City of New Orleans. The older Lower Garden District and later Garden District are the principal divisions of the former City of Lafayette. A landmark of the Lower Garden District is the Margaret memorial at Margaret Place, shown here c. 1890. As the first public monument erected to a woman in the U.S., it memorializes philanthropist Margaret Haughery (1813–1882), benefactress of the city's orphaned children.

The Garden District's principal thoroughfare is St. Charles Avenue, which extends out from the CBD to Carrollton Avenue in a great curve following the crescent-shaped bend of the upriver flow of the Mississippi. In the CBD the road is St. Charles Street, but uptown from Lee Circle it becomes St. Charles Avenue. This 1904 view depicts a Confederate Veterans parade on lower St. Charles Avenue, just up from Lee Circle. None of these houses still stand.

Originally called Tivoli Place, Lee Circle was renamed in 1883 in memory of Gen. Robert E. Lee, whose statue crowns the column. The building at right was the Bienville Hotel. This image is from the 1930s.

This 1940s photograph captures the view looking down St. Charles Street into the CBD from Lee Circle. Lee's bronze statue stands 16.5 feet tall atop a marble column 60 feet high. The monument was dedicated February 22, 1884, and cost $40,000. The sculptor was Alexander Doyle, who also created the Margaret memorial nearby. In the distance the Hibernia National Bank Building stands out prominently just to the right of the Lee column.

Near Lee Circle, on Carondelet Street at Calliope, stood Temple Sinai (above), built in 1872. In 1928 the congregation moved to a new site on St. Charles Avenue near Tulane and Loyola Universities. The old temple continued in use as a theater until it was razed in 1977. On Constance Street, some dozen blocks into the Lower Garden District from Lee Circle, stands St. Alphonsus Catholic Church (below), one of many important church edifices in the city. It was built in 1855.

Once a landmark of Howard Avenue, the Delord-Sarpy Mansion (pictured above) was one of the last old plantation houses to remain standing in New Orleans. Built in 1813, it was the oldest building above Canal Street when it was demolished in 1957 to build an approach to the Mississippi River Bridge. The same approach was closed and eliminated in the mid-1990s. Howard Avenue was still called Delord Street in the 1850s when the Italianate mansion below was built. In 1887, the era of the photo, the mansion became the first home of Sophie Newcomb Women's College, now part of Tulane University.

While the Lower Garden District lies on the river side of St. Charles, the Central City neighborhood lies along the lake side. The area was once a largely Irish neighborhood whose development began in the 1830s. Later a substantial influx of Germans settled here, and in the 19th century a large portion of the city's vibrant Jewish community lived in the area. Above are two Victorian double shotgun houses of a style typical in Central City. Below is the Laurel School, typical of New Orleans public schools of the turn of the 20th century. It was built in 1897 at 833 Philip Street.

Throughout Central City, the Lower Garden District, and even the Garden District, there are numerous once-elegant 19th-century homes now falling into a state of ruin. While decayed mansions such as the one above on Carondelet Street appear romantic in photographs, they are a blight to the neighborhoods in which they stand, and their decay and frequent demolition is the source of irreparable loss to the city. One vestige of the past still very much alive is the St. Charles Avenue streetcar, begun in 1835. Electrified in 1893, the cars running today are 1920s models, such as the one seen below in a mid-1920s photo. This is the oldest continuously operating streetcar line in the world.

The residence of Capt. Thomas P. Leathers on Carondelet at Josephine Streets is one of the best-preserved mansions remaining on the lake side of St. Charles. Captain Leathers built and commanded seven steamboats called *Natchez* during his 57-year career on the Mississippi, piloting the *Natchez* in its famous 1870 race with the *Robt. E. Lee*. He appears at left on the upper balcony of the house he built in 1859. He died here in 1896 after being struck by a hit-and-run bicyclist on St. Charles Avenue while crossing at St. Andrew Street. He is buried in the City Cemetery of Natchez, Mississippi. The house stands next door to the one pictured at the top of p. 113.

The Mississippi River Bridge is visible from the Pontchartrain Hotel, a landmark of the Garden District since the 1920s. The Pontchartrain was originally built as an apartment hotel and its suites have been a home away from home to many celebrities from the world over. It has been said, without exaggeration, that the Pontchartrain, Roosevelt, and Monteleone Hotels are to 20th-century New Orleans what the St. Charles and St. Louis Hotels were to the city in the 19th century. The Pontchartrain's restaurant, the French Room, is regarded as one of the city's finest. The view here is of the Lower Garden District and the Mississippi as seen from the Pontchartrain's roof.

This unusual structure stands directly across the street from the Pontchartrain Hotel at the downtown river corner of St. Charles Avenue and Josephine Street. It is the original top portion of the Eiffel Tower, removed and replaced during renovations and brought to New Orleans in conjunction with the 1984 World's Fair. Since then it has variously served as a restaurant, bar, and reception hall. This view is toward the Mississippi with Josephine Street on the right.

The Trinity Episcopal Church on Jackson Avenue and Coliseum Street was built in 1852, although the main entrance was remodeled and the tower added in 1873. The Reverend Leonidas Polk, cousin of U.S. president James Knox Polk, was at one time the rector of this congregation, founded in 1847. During the antebellum period, as the bishop of Louisiana, Polk founded numerous churches throughout the state. He also helped to found the University of the South at Sewanee, Tennessee. Serving as a Confederate general, Bishop Polk was killed in action in Georgia in 1864. In the 1940s his remains were transferred to Christ Church Cathedral on St. Charles Avenue, where they rest today.

Another historic Garden District church is the Jackson Avenue Evangelical Church, located on Jackson Avenue at Chippewa Street. Noted particularly for its brickwork, the church still stands, though now minus the upper portion of its corner tower. Jackson Avenue is commonly regarded as the boundary between the Lower Garden District and the Garden District.

This view of St. Charles Avenue was taken in the 1910s. St. Charles Avenue and Washington, Prytania, Coliseum, Chestnut, and Magazine Streets are among the Garden District's most important roads.

Jefferson Davis died on December 6, 1889, in the Garden District home of Judge Charles Erasmus Fenner, a close friend of Davis at the time of his death. The home, shown here in the 1930s, was built in 1849 at 1134 First Street.

The home of novelist Anne Rice is located at 1239 First Street. Built in 1857, it has been the residence of several families through the years, including that of U.S. Judge John Minor Wisdom from 1947 to 1972. For a time the house was known as "Rosegate." It has been the Rice residence since 1990.

"Cornstalk" fences, made by the Wood & Miltenberger foundry (the New Orleans division of Philadelphia's Wood & Perot), are rare today because of their original high cost. Apocryphal stories have developed about these fences, though none with any basis in reality. Pictured here are two views of a fine example from around the Italianate mansion built by Col. Robert Short at 1448 Fourth Street, corner with Prytania, in 1859. A better known, though somewhat less imposing, example of the same fence type can be found at 915 Royal Street in the French Quarter, the Victorian residence of the late State Supreme Court Justice F.X. Martin. Yet another may be found on North White Street in the Bayou St. John area, and fragments of similar fences exist elsewhere in the city. After the surrender of New Orleans in 1862, federal authorities seized the Short villa to be the executive mansion for the occupation government.

An especially noteworthy Garden District mansion is the residence of sugar planter Bradish Johnson, built in 1872 at 2343 Prytania. In 1929 it became home to the Louise S. McGehee School, a private school for girls, and remains so still.

A short distance away is Lafayette Cemetery Number One, located at 1400 Washington Avenue, just opposite the noteworthy Commander's Palace Restaurant. The cemetery was established in 1833 and contains many important 19th-century tombs.

Beyond the Garden District, St. Charles Avenue passes through the Uptown and University sections of New Orleans. An Uptown landmark on St. Charles is the Touro Synagogue, built between 1904 and 1907. Founded in 1827, it is the oldest Jewish congregation in the United States outside the original 13 colonies. This photograph shows the ornate detail of the synagogue's architecture.

Another St. Charles Avenue landmark was the Jewish Orphans Home, founded in 1855. The building shown here was dedicated in 1886 at St. Charles and Jefferson Avenues. Today this site is the location of the main New Orleans Jewish Community Center, the oldest of the city's two Jewish Community Centers.

This uptown view of St. Charles Avenue was captured looking from the neutral ground toward downtown around 1900. By the time this photograph was made, this area had become known for its fabulous post-Civil War mansions. A variety of architectural styles can be found in these great homes, many of which survive, although many were lost to development in the mid-20th century. Queen Anne Victorian, Italianate, Romanesque Revival, and Richardson Romanesque are the most commonly seen types. The Richardson Romanesque style was developed by St. James Parish native Henry Hobson Richardson, whose short career (he died in 1886 at the age of 48) was one of the most influential in American architecture. Richardson, who grew up in New Orleans, lived and worked in Boston but his designs influenced architecture nationally. A Richardson Romanesque house is visible second from the left in this photograph.

This was the stately residence of Tom Anderson, oilman, state legislator, and onetime boss of Storyville, New Orleans's legal red light district. Clearly influenced by Richardson, the house stands in a pristine state of turn-of-the-20th-century preservation at the corner of St. Charles Avenue and Valence Street. Anderson died in 1931 at age 70; his widow, former Storyville madam Gertrude Dix, died in 1961 at age 87.

This is just one of the great oak trees of Audubon Park, which opened in 1871 on a site combining parts of the Bore and Foucher plantations. It was on this plantation that Etienne de Bore first successfully granulated sugar. This image is from 1930 but the oaks, some of them centuries old, still remain.

In 1884 the World's Fair and Centennial Cotton Exposition was held in New Orleans, its pavilions occupying the modern site of Audubon Park. The exposition's opening address, portrayed in the engraving above, was given on behalf of the President of the Unites States, Chester Alan Arthur. Few remnants of the fair remain today, with the notable exception of a large meteorite that was on exhibit and proved to heavy to move afterward. The park was established in 1871 and later named for Louisiana ornithologist and artist John James Audubon. Today, among numerous other amenities, the park is home to the Audubon Zoo, regarded as one of the nation's top city zoos.

The campus of Tulane University is located across St. Charles Avenue from Audubon Park. Tulane was the successor to the University of Louisiana, founded in 1847. In 1884 Paul Tulane, a former New Orleans merchant then residing in Princeton, New Jersey, endowed the school so generously as to virtually recreate it. Thus, ever since it has borne his name. In 1891 a portion of the Foucher plantation was acquired as a new campus, as the old one on Common Street (now Tulane Avenue) had been outgrown. In 1894 the first three buildings were constructed, including the one shown here, now Gibson Hall, photographed a year after its completion. Gibson Hall is named for Randall Lee Gibson, first president of the college's board of administrators.

Nearly adjacent to Tulane's campus is that of Loyola University of the South, established in 1904 and incorporated as a university in 1912. Today Loyola is the largest Roman Catholic university in the United States, south of St. Louis. This is a mid-1920s view of Loyola's Marquette Hall, built in 1911.

This 1990s photograph shows Joseph Street at Prytania. The sign is a joke, but has been in place for a number of years. Its reference is to New Orleans' infamous cockroaches, which, like mosquitoes, thrive in the hot, humid, tropical climate. Shared space with insects is a small price to pay for the rich, unique, and pleasant lifestyle that the city of New Orleans has to offer.

A fine 1890s Queen Anne residence on Magazine Street undergoes restoration in the 1990s. The renewal of old homes and commercial buildings is working wonders in preserving the valuable and special architectural and social heritage of New Orleans. Organizations such as the Preservation Resource Center of New Orleans and Operation Comeback have made great strides in the later 20th-century renewal of New Orleans' historic neighborhoods, helping to ensure that the historic ambiance of the Crescent City remains for future generations of New Orleanians and visitors to enjoy and cherish.

ACKNOWLEDGMENTS

I wish to express particular thanks to the staff of the Historic New Orleans Collection, Williams Research Center; the University of New Orleans Library, Special Collections Division; Louisiana State University in Shreveport, Noel Memorial Library Department of Archives and Special Collections; the Louisiana State Library; and the New Orleans Public Library. I also wish to express a special thank you to my friend Gaspar J. "Buddy" Stall, whose knowledge of New Orleans history is phenomenal. Likewise, a special note of acknowledgement is due to the late Leonard V. Huber and Al Rose, whose extraordinary knowledge of the Crescent City's history has been an inspiration and a resource; I am privileged to have known them.

Except as noted below, historic images used in this book are from prints, negatives, or engravings in the collection of the author. Other images are reproduced through the kind courtesy of the following:

The Archives National de France, p. 11 (top and bottom); The Historic New Orleans Collection, p. 82 (bottom); the Library of Congress, p. 42 (bottom); the Louisiana State Museum, pp. 13 (top), 21, 26 (top), 45, 46 (bottom), 63 (top), and 88; Louisiana State University in Shreveport, the Noel Memorial Library Department of Archives and Special Collections, pp. 56, 70 (top and bottom), 74 (top), 75 (top), 76 (top), 77, and 110 (bottom); the Museum of Fine Arts, City of Pau, p. 67; the New Orleans Public Library, p. 108 (top); and the U.S. Army Military Research Institute, p. 33.

Photographs by Eric J. Brock appear as follows: pp. 12 (bottom), 16 (bottom), 24 (bottom), 25 (top and bottom), 27 (top), 31 (bottom), 32 (top), 34 (top and bottom), 41 (top), 57, 59 (bottom), 62 (bottom), 63 (bottom), 81 (bottom), 82 (top), 91 (top), 93 (bottom), 101, 104 (top and bottom), 105, 106, 115 (top and bottom), 118 (bottom), 119 (top and bottom), 120 (top and bottom), 121 (top), 123 (top), and 127 (top and bottom).

Engravings originally appearing in contemporary publications are as follows: *The Century Magazine*, p. 46 (top) and 64 (bottom); *Frank Leslie's Illustrated News*, p. 47; *Harper's Weekly*, p. 36 (top), 51 (top), 71, and 72 (top); *Illustrated American*, p. 65 (top); *Jewell's Crescent City Illustrated*, p. 38 (top); and *Scribner's*, p. 65 (bottom).

About the Author

Eric J. Brock is a writer, historian, and the author of several books on Louisiana subjects. A graduate of Centenary College of Louisiana, he is an editorial page writer for the *Shreveport Journal* and is active in historic preservation efforts, particularly in New Orleans and Shreveport, between which he divides his time. Among his books are four others published by Arcadia: *New Orleans Cemeteries, Images of America: Shreveport, Shreveport in the Twentieth Century*, and, with Gary D. Joiner, *Red River Steamboats*.